EXPLORING WORLD CULTURES

# Myanmar

Laura L. Sullivan

Cavendish
Square
New York

Published in 2019 by Cavendish Square Publishing, LLC
243 5th Avenue, Suite 136, New York, NY 10016

Copyright © 2019 by Cavendish Square Publishing, LLC

First Edition

Website: cavendishsq.com

This publication represents the opinions and views of the author based on his or her personal experience, knowledge, and research. The information in this book serves as a general guide only. The author and publisher have used their best efforts in preparing this book and disclaim liability rising directly or indirectly from the use and application of this book.

All websites were available and accurate when this book was sent to press.

Library of Congress Cataloging-in-Publication Data

Names: Sullivan, Laura L., 1974- author.
Title: Myanmar / Laura L. Sullivan.
Description: First edition. | New York : Cavendish Square, 2018. |
Series: Exploring world cultures | Includes bibliographical references and index.
Identifiers: LCCN 2018021430 (print) | LCCN 2018021668 (ebook) |
ISBN 9781502643490 (ebook) | ISBN 9781502643483 (library bound) |
ISBN 9781502643469 (pbk) | ISBN 9781502643476 (6 pack)
Subjects: LCSH: Burma—Juvenile literature.
Classification: LCC DS527.4 (ebook) | LCC DS527.4 .S95 2018 (print) | DDC 959.1--dc23
LC record available at https://lccn.loc.gov/2018021430

Editorial Director: David McNamara
Editor: Lauren Miller
Copy Editor: Nathan Heidelberger
Associate Art Director: Alan Sliwinski
Designer: Christina Shults
Production Coordinator: Karol Szymczuk
Photo Research: J8 Media

Printed in the United States of America

# Contents

# Introduction

Myanmar is located in Southeast Asia. It was once named Burma. Myanmar has beautiful forests and lots of wildlife. It also has natural resources. Oil and jade are two examples. Myanmar is home to around fifty-five million people.

There have been many problems in Myanmar's past. Violence between **ethnic groups** caused **civil war**. Until 2011, the military ruled the country. Some groups are still fighting today, but conditions have improved in many places. Despite many problems, there is hope that one day there will be peace.

The people of Myanmar still enjoy life. Sports like soccer and dancing are popular. The people eat many delicious foods. They celebrate many traditions and enjoy festivals.

There is much to learn about the country of Myanmar.

Most Burmese people live normal lives despite conflicts in some parts of the country.

# Geography

Myanmar is located in Southeast Asia. It borders China to the north. Laos and Thailand are east of Myanmar. India and Bangladesh are to the west. To the south and west, Myanmar's coast touches two bodies of water. They are the Bay of Bengal and the Andaman Sea. The country is about 261,200 square miles (676,500 square kilometers).

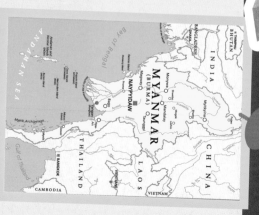

This map shows Myanmar's location and neighbors.

## FACT!

Myanmar's highest mountains have lots of snow.

## Rainy Days

The wettest parts of Myanmar get up to 200 inches (508 centimeters) of rain every year.

The Irrawaddy is Myanmar's longest river.

Myanmar has several mountain ranges. They all run north to south through the country. The tallest mountain is called Hkakabo Razi. There are also three major rivers. They are the Salween, the Sittaung, and the Irrawaddy. Near the rivers are flatlands. Lots of farming is done there.

The climate is hot and tropical. Myanmar gets **monsoons,** or seasons of very heavy rain.

# History

Modern humans came to Myanmar around eleven thousand years ago. Later on, they made some of the first bronze tools and weapons.

For a long time, different groups wanted to rule Myanmar. Empires collapsed and reunified many times. Later, the Portuguese, French, and British all tried to control

This Buddhist temple is over two thousand years old.

## FACT!

Myanmar was once called Burma. The military changed the name in 1989. Both names come from the Burman, or Bamar, people.

# A World-Famous Leader

Aung San Suu Kyi is a leader in the democracy movement. She won the Nobel Peace Prize in 1991.

Aung San Suu Kyi helped guide Myanmar toward democracy.

Myanmar. The British East India Company was very interested in Myanmar's natural resources. In 1886, the British took control. Myanmar did not become an independent country until 1948.

In 1962, the military took over the country. However, in 2007, Buddhist monks led the push for less military control. Today, Myanmar is struggling to become a **democracy.**

The capital city of Myanmar is Naypyidaw. Before 2006, the capital was Yangon (also called Rangoon).

Myanmar is a parliamentary republic. That means there is a president and a **parliament**. It is called the Assembly of the Union. The people elect 75 percent of the members that serve in the assembly. The military appoints the other 25 percent.

The Assembly of the Union meets here.

In 2015, Aung San Suu Kyi's political party won the majority. This party has been pushing strongly for more democracy. They also want a smaller role for the military. Right now, Myanmar's government is split between military rule and true democracy.

A parliament meeting in session.

## Ongoing Conflict

In Myanmar, many groups have fought with each other since 1948. It is the world's longest-running civil war.

# The Economy

Myanmar is very poor. Many citizens do not have a good education. There are few factories in Myanmar. There is little focus on technology. The country has little to sell to other countries.

Farming is the largest industry. Rice is the main crop. Beans, sugarcane, and livestock are also raised. About 65 percent of people in Myanmar work in farming.

Ruby miners work in harsh conditions.

**FACT!**

The currency in Myanmar is called the Burmese kyat. As of April 2018, 1 US dollar was equal to 1,322 Burmese kyats.

Fishing is also common. Fish are caught in the sea and in rivers. Myanmar has many forests. Teak and ironwood trees are cut down and sold as timber.

Burmese kyats are colorful.

Mining is another important industry. Many gems are mined there. Myanmar produces 90 percent of the rubies sold around the world.

## Tourism

Tourism in Myanmar is slowly growing. In 2012, more than one million tourists visited Myanmar. They come for the beaches, wildlife, and beautiful **pagodas**.

# The Environment

The forests of
Myanmar are full of
life. Animals like tigers,
leopards, elephants,
rhinoceroses, and
monkeys live there.
They also have cobras,
crocodiles, and pythons
near the rivers. However,
logging is destroying these areas. Rules have
been set up to try to stop this.

Snub-nosed monkeys are
easy to spot!

**FACT!**

The snub-nosed monkey lives in the forests. Its
nose turns up, so it sneezes when it rains!

# Elephants at Work

Trained elephants help take teak trees out of Myanmar's forests. They replace machines that can make the air polluted.

Teak wood harvested by elephants is very valuable.

Overfishing is a problem in Myanmar's rivers and along the coast. New buildings have also hurt the mangrove trees that grow there.

Myanmar has terrible air pollution. It is caused by wood fires used for cooking and power plants that burn coal. Old cars and buses also add to pollution. Today, more people are moving to big cities. Cities are becoming crowded and dirty.

# The People Today

There are 135 different ethnic groups living in Myanmar. The Burman, or Bamar, are the largest group. They make up about 68 percent of the population. Other ethnic groups include the Rohingya, Shan, Karen, and Rakhine groups.

Myanmar is very divided. Ethnic groups often stay together. People are also separated by money.

Children are important and taken care of in Burmese families.

## The Rohingya

The Rohingya follow the Muslim faith. They have faced violence, starvation, and **persecution** in Myanmar. Recently, up to one million Rohingya have left Myanmar. Many live in Bangladesh as refugees.

Many people are very poor. A small number of people have lots of money.

People in Myanmar tend to have big social communities. Families are big and very close. Even distant cousins and great aunts are considered as close as brothers and sisters. They usually live in the same village or region.

The people of Myanmar are friendly. However, they usually don't like to show too much emotion in public.

# Lifestyle

People in Myanmar believe that as you grow older, you become wiser. The elderly, parents, and teachers are highly respected.

Women in Myanmar have legal rights. They can choose whom to marry. They can divorce

Women and men both wear wrap-around sarongs.

## FACT!

A sarong is a long piece of fabric. It is wrapped around the body. Both men and women wear it like a dress or a skirt.

## Face Painting

*Thanaka* is a white paste used to decorate the skin. Women and girls paint designs on their faces and arms. Sometimes men and boys do too.

Here is an example of *thanaka* decorations.

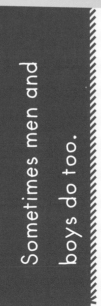

their husbands and own property. Both men and women are usually allowed to work the same jobs.

Socially, men have more power. At parties, women are usually separate from men. At dinner, men are served first. A man is considered the head of a household.

# Religion

Myanmar is a land of many different beliefs. Around 87 percent of people are Buddhist. Some people instead practice religions like Islam, Christianity, and Hinduism. Often non-Buddhists are treated unfairly. For example, sometimes they cannot work in the government or military.

Most Buddhists follow Theravada Buddhism. They believe that when a person dies, they are reborn into another life. The goal is to end this cycle of rebirth by achieving nirvana. This is a state without desire, hate, or ignorance.

These boys are training to become Buddhist monks.

## FACT!

Nats are spirits with names. They have shrines throughout Myanmar.

Muslims in Myanmar worship at mosques.

Most villages have a Buddhist monastery. Most families also have a shrine in their home. The shrine usually has a statue of Buddha on a throne.

# Faith Communities

It is very uncommon in Myanmar to change religions. This is because communities practice the same religion. Marriage between people of two different religions does not happen a lot.

# Language

Around one hundred different languages are spoken in Myanmar. The official language is Burmese. Other languages widely spoken include Karen, Shan, Kachin, Mon, and Chin.

Burmese is written using mostly circles and half circles.

## FACT!

Burmese has two forms. Formal speech is used when speaking with someone older. Informal speech is casual and more relaxed. It is used when speaking with someone of the same age or younger.

## Learning Burmese

Kids often learn to read and write Burmese in schools run by Buddhist monks. Later, they learn Burmese and English in government-run schools.

Some languages are only spoken in small villages or tribes. The government discourages the use of those languages. Some have been lost.

Burmese is related to Chinese and other smaller languages. English is often taught as a second language in school. Today, English is used by the upper class and in the government.

# Arts and Festivals

Dance, music, and crafts are all important in Myanmar. Buddhism influences many artists in Myanmar. Many artists make beautiful statues of Buddha.

Other common crafts include painting and making gold jewelry.

Dancers perform stories and plays at local festivals.

## Traditional Dance

Dance in Myanmar has been heavily influenced by traditions from Thailand. The dances are performed in beautiful costumes and usually focus on poses rather than just movement.

Storytelling is also popular. Other religions influence storytelling. The folktale *Yama Zatdaw* is a retelling of the Hindu story *Ramayana*.

One type of festival in Myanmar is the pagoda festival. It is a multiday celebration that is similar to a fair. Often there are markets, dancing, and music.

# Fun and Play

Soccer, also called football, is one of the most popular sports in Myanmar. It is played in almost every village. There are professional teams too.

The Burmese professional soccer team.

Chinlone is the country's national sport. It is also called caneball. It is played with a woven rattan ball. The ball feels similar to a basket. Players stand in a circle and pass the ball to each

## Martial Arts

Myanmar has several forms of martial arts. They include *bando, lethwei, banshay, and pongyi-thaing.*

Chinlone is played with light, woven balls like these.

other without using their hands. If the ball touches the ground, the game is over. People of all ages play chinlone.

Chinlone is an art form as well as a sport. It is influenced by the martial arts and dances of Myanmar.

# Food

Burmese food has influences from Thailand, China, and India. Fish is used in many recipes. *Ngapi* is used in many dishes. It is a paste made from shrimp or fish. Fish sauce is also common.

The national dish of Myanmar is *mohinga*. It is a fish soup served

Mohinga can be made at home or bought as street food.

with rice noodles. It is topped with lime, cilantro, onions, and chilies. It used to be served for breakfast. It is so popular now that it is eaten throughout the day.

Most meals have rice. Usually it is steamed and served plain with several side dishes. Curried chicken or fish are popular. Meals often include soup too. Vegetables may be boiled or served in a salad.

## Drinks in Myanmar

Drinks aren't usually served with a meal. Instead, liquid comes from broth in the food. However, green tea is a popular drink in Myanmar.

# Glossary

**civil war**    A war between citizens of the same country.

**constitution**    A document that outlines the laws of a nation.

**democracy**    A form of government where the power lies with the people, through elections.

**ethnic group**    People who share a common background or culture.

**monsoon**    A seasonal period of very heavy rain.

**pagoda**    A Buddhist temple.

**parliament**    A group elected by the people of a country to make laws.

**persecution**    Being treated poorly because of one's ethnicity, religion, or beliefs.

# Find Out More

## Books

King, Dedie. *I See the Sun in Myanmar.* Hardwick, MA: Satya House Publications, 2013.

Rush, Elizabeth. *M is for Myanmar.* San Francisco: ThingsAsian Press: 2011

## Website

**Ducksters: Burma (Myanmar)**

http://www.ducksters.com/geography/country.php?country=Burma

## Video

**Thirst Aid Myanmar**

https://www.youtube.com/watch?v=QajmnDn78-g

# Index

Buddhism, 9, 20–21, 23–24

civil war, 4, 11

constitution, 10

democracy, 9, 11

ethnic group, 4, 16

farming, 7, 12

military, 4, 8–11, 20

monsoon, 7

pagoda, 13, 25

parliament, 10

persecution, 17

Rohingya, 16–17

# About the Author

**Laura L. Sullivan** is the author of more than forty fiction and nonfiction books, including the fantasies *Under the Green Hill* and *Guardian of the Green Hill*. Sullivan lives in Florida, where she likes to bike, hike, kayak, hunt fossils, and practice Brazilian jiujitsu.